BUT I TRUST THE SCHOLARS

WHICH BIBLE SCHOLARS DO YOU TRUST?

DAVID W. DANIELS

For a complete list of distributors near you,
call (909) 987-0771, or visit **www.chick.com**

Copyright © 2019 David W. Daniels

Published by:
CHICK PUBLICATIONS
PO Box 3500, Ontario, Calif. 91761-1019 USA
Tel: (909) 987-0771
Fax: (909) 941-8128
Web: www.chick.com
Email: postmaster@chick.com

First Printing

Printed in the United States of America

All rights reserved. No part of this book may be reproduced, stored in a retrieval system or transmitted in any form or by any means (electronic, mechanical, photocopying, recording or otherwise) without permission in writing from the copyright owner.
Art by Deborah Daniels, Jack Chick and Fred Carter

ISBN: 978-0-75891-2978

Contents

Introduction 4

1 Early Bible Scholars 6

2 Lucifer, Scholar Of Doubt 12

3 Jesus The Master Scholar 16

4 New Testament Scholars 18

5 Early Church Fathers 21

6 Two Types of Scholars; Two Agendas 26

7 Early Church Scholars 33

8 Warfare Against the "Good Guy" Scholars 39

9 Truth Explodes 43

10 The Counter-Reformation:
 A New Kind of Attack 46

11 Motives Of The Scholars
 Behind The Modern Bible Versions 62

12 Real World Seminary Scholars 68

13 Summary 72

Introduction

Often, in the discussion related to Bible versions, you may hear these words pop out: "But I trust the scholars."

But there's more than one kind of scholar, just like there's more than one kind of person. Some people you can trust with your life, and others you wouldn't trust to help you cross the street. We must ask: "Are we trusting the *right* scholars?" Well, how many kinds of scholars *are* there? And what difference does it make, which kind we trust? Isn't it enough that they are scholars?

Because there are two streams of Bible history, as I showed in ***Did the Catholic Church Give Us the Bible?***,[1] they produce two kinds of scholars with two different agendas. One kind was dedicated to preserving accurate translations of exact copies of the original writings. The other kind was dedicated to using the scriptures as a vehicle to promote their own questionable agenda. So we end up with two *methods* of scholarship based on two very different ***agendas.***

The one began from fear of God's commands not to tamper with His words (See Deuteronomy 4:2; Proverbs 30:6), and trust that God would keep His promise to preserve His

---

1) *Did the Catholic Church Give Us the Bible?* (Chick Publications, 2005), chapter 2.

words through the generations of copies and translations (See Matthew 24:35; Mark 13:31; and Luke 21:33).

The other ignores the warnings, doubting that we could have accurate copies, or else that God would keep His promise. This book will give enough of a general outline of the competing histories to illustrate for you the two different agendas. Details can be found in the other books that I have written on Bible versions.

Chapter 1

Early Bible Scholars

In the beginning, God made man with a built-in language. We can see this in Genesis, when it records God's conversations with Adam as they strolled together in the Garden of Eden. And since he created Adam perfectly, and there were no audio recorders, it is therefore probable that he was able to ***write.***

If there were writers of history, then from the beginning there were scholars. Scholars are educated people. They are not necessarily people who wrote books of the Bible. But think about this: **Somebody** wrote Genesis 1. The only one there at the time was God —and the only way the author could have written it is if God Himself had *told* him what He did!

It makes sense that Adam was the first author, since he's the guy God gave everything to in the beginning. He must have had a clear intellectual mind, being perfect and all. And we are descended from him, and at least some of us have intellectual minds. Adam was also smart enough to name all the animals.

We know that others were able to write and record information, as well. How else could we know private conversations Abraham had with those around him? **Someone** had to write them down at some point. And then once written, those words had to be passed down to the next generation.

It is possible that before the fall they had perfect memory.

But when death entered the picture, written records became necessary. They created records of what God said and what man did. Perhaps they realized that what they did had clear consequences (See Genesis 3:15-19).

ADAM

Adam began to write down what God had told them and what had happened before, in their lost paradise. Adam lived 930 years, long enough to see his great, great, great, great, great, great grandson, Lamech, Noah's father.[2] That means Adam was able to chronicle 800 years of civilization outside the garden.

All of what we call civilization, requires written instructions and records. The civilized world is too complex to rely on oral communication alone.

In fact, the term "these are the generations" in Genesis are considered by many to be a marker of the next generation's writer taking over and telling about the people around his time. In fact, Genesis 5 begins, "This is *the book of* the generations of Adam." And that was *before the flood!*

MOSES

Moses compiled ancient histories for what became the book of Genesis.

---

2) See *Babylon Religion* (Chick Publications, 2006), p. 17.

When we look into known history for the earliest Bible scholars, Moses comes to the top. We know from the Bible that he was much more than a prophet. God made sure he was educated in some of the finest schools of the most powerful nation at his time. Moses was a scholar, a thinker:

"And Moses was learned in all the wisdom of the Egyptians, and was mighty in words and in deeds," Acts 7:22. God used that to prepare him to write the first Torah scroll, Genesis-Deuteronomy.

But for the form of his writings, and the histories preserved by God's people, he surely was standing on the shoulders of scholars who faithfully preserved the history of God's dealings with man before Moses' time.

We know that God did not dictate the early chapters of Genesis to Moses. In Genesis 2 is this passage:

> Genesis 2:11-14: The name of the first is Pison: that is it which compasseth the whole land of Havilah, where there is gold; And the gold of that land is good: there is bdellium and the onyx stone. And the name of the second river is Gihon: the same is it that compasseth the whole land of Ethiopia. And the name of the third river is Hiddekel: that is it which goeth toward the east of Assyria. And the fourth river is Euphrates.

Neither the Pison nor the Gihon is around to this day. However, they were clearly there before the flood. And whoever wrote this noted, in the ***present tense,*** that they *compass* either Havilah or Ethiopia. They didn't *after* the flood. But they clearly did, *before* the flood. Anyone who wrote the present tense after the flood would be a liar. And anyone before the flood who didn't know this to be true would have called the writer a liar.

So the only option is that someone before the flood knew this was true, and everyone else knew it was true. So it was written down, in the **present tense**. Then the tablets with this information were passed down, until they came into the hands of God's scholar, Moses.

It is likely, however, that written records were stored in a library in the living quarters of Noah's ark and later combined with various records of the descendants of Noah (Genesis 6:9), Terah (11:27), Ishmael (25:12), Isaac (25:19), Esau (36:1) and Jacob (37:2). Moses, then, included them with his own record of the Exodus and Levitical Law, their travels (Numbers) and his own second giving of the law (Deuteronomy).

Again, God picked out a world-class scholar, Moses, to permanently record for future generations this early segment of world history. Moses' scholarship responsibilities were then passed on to one of the tribes of Israel, the Levites.

Levites

> Deuteronomy 31:24-26: And it came to pass, when Moses had made an end of writing the words of this law in a book, until they were finished, That **Moses commanded the Levites**, which bare the ark of the covenant of the LORD, saying, Take this book of the law, and put it in the side of the ark of the covenant of the LORD your God, that it may be there for a witness against thee.

The Levitical priests were free from menial labor to promote God's agenda of reconciliation of mankind. Thus they became a scholarly class, tasked with studying, copying, preserving and teaching God's words.

> Deuteronomy 24:8: "Take heed in the plague of leprosy, that thou observe diligently, and do according to all that the priests the Levites shall teach you: *as I commanded them, so ye shall observe to do.*"

Even the kings were required by God to be scholars.

> Deuteronomy 17:18: "And it shall be, when he [the king] sitteth upon the throne of his kingdom, that *he shall write him a copy of this law* in a book out of that which is before the priests the Levites:"

Prophets and Kings

Despite the jumble of judges, and corruptions of kings, more of God's words were preserved through His prophets, poet-prophets like King David, and recorded wisdom given to Solomon and others. There was never a time when God failed to set His words before His people.

> Jeremiah 7:25: "Since the day that your fathers came forth out of the land of Egypt unto this day I have even sent unto you all my servants the prophets, daily rising up early and sending them:"

We have many of those very words, because God made sure they wrote them down. The books of Samuel and Kings are a perfect example of the writings of prophets, in addition to the Prophetic books (Isaiah-Malachi). And the books of the Chronicles are the writings of faithful Levitical priests.

Micah and other prophets gave God's words to largely disinterested crowds, not unlike today's street preachers.

By the time of Jesus, we had a blessing that came only by the providence of God.

Families had carefully copied the Hebrew scriptures for so long and so carefully, that no one could dispute the text. Synagogues had their own copies of the scriptures all over Israel. If there were a difference between texts, anyone visiting would know it. God used this to preserve the accuracy of the Hebrew scriptures. As a result, all the unbelieving scholars could do was argue about it.

Chapter 2

Lucifer, Scholar Of Doubt

But there was another line of scholars with a totally opposite agenda. And you might recognize their top expert. He used a serpent's body and turned Eve into the first Bible critic.

Perversion can only be done to what is genuine. To pervert is to "turn about," to change from its original form or purpose. The Devil cannot create anything. He can only pervert what is already created and, in this case, preserved: the holy words of the living God.

The history of preservation was overseen by God. But there was another history, dedicated to the *perVERsion* of God's words, in contrast to *preservation*. And it didn't start with God. Nor did it start with man. It started with the father of lies himself, the Devil.

It stares us in the face in the eyes of the serpent who spoke to Eve in the garden of Eden, Paradise itself. This serpent spoke words so simple that they turned confidence into confusion. And it only took one question: **"Yea, hath God said…?"** (Genesis 3:1)

That moved Eve and her husband onto a four-step descent into chaos: *Confusion* about what God said. *Doubt* about whether God said it. *Disbelief* about whether those words were God's, after all. *Rebellion*, rejecting the words of God, and deciding to do things ***their way.*** This is the same course that every Bible-doubting scholar has ever taken.

That doubt eventually corrupted the entire world population. And because of the resulting rebellion, God destroyed the world and started all over again, with Noah and his little family.

Neither Moses, nor any of the prophets, was ever able to completely purge that doubt from the children of Israel. They repeatedly strayed to the local idols. But even in the darkest days of Israel's idolatry, God had a remnant who ***preserved*** His words.

The scribes and the lawyers In Jesus' day were charged with maintaining the purity of the basic text of the Hebrew Scriptures. When Jesus rightly called them out for their sin, it was never for **changing** the Scriptures, only for *reinterpreting* them to suit their agenda.

By the first century AD, these scholars had evolved themselves into a scholarly class, and set themselves apart from and above others. These were the ***scribes***, who kept arguing with Jesus during His ministry. But God made sure that these doubters and debaters wrote all their disputes into other books ***—not the Bible!***

The Hebrews were so set in their ways about passing down the words of God, it left no room for tampering. Records of these scholars' doubts and disputes are preserved to this day in two sets of volumes: the Babylonian Talmud and the Jerusalem Talmud, as well as other books.

Therefore, if the unbelieving scholars wanted to write their crazy ideas and theories *into a Bible's text*, it would have had to be in another language. ***And that's exactly what they did.*** In Alexandria, Egypt especially, apostate Jewish scholars tried to blend Greek language and philosophy, and their own speculations, with the scriptures.

The result is the jumbled mess we call the Septuagint. And it led to a lot of embarrassing results. For example, Methuselah, whose name is said to mean "His death shall bring it," *died the very year of the flood*, in the Hebrew text. But in the Septuagint, Methuselah *lived 14 years after the flood*. What was he doing? Hanging onto the side of the ark? Nope. The scripture is clear:

> Genesis 7:21-24: "And all flesh died that moved upon the earth, both of fowl, and of cattle, and of beast, and of every creeping thing that creepeth upon the earth, and every man: All in whose nostrils was the breath of life, of all that was in the dry land, died. And every living substance was destroyed which was upon the face of the ground, **both man**, and cattle, and the creeping things, and the fowl of the heaven; and they were destroyed from the earth: and Noah only remained alive, and they that were with him in the ark. And the waters prevailed upon the earth an hundred and fifty days."

No land-dwelling, air-breathing creature survived outside the ark. It was inside, or death. The Septuagint is completely wrong and proven to be a fake translation of the holy words of God. If you want to know more, read my book *Did Jesus Use the Septuagint?*[3]

The Lord made sure that the one thing they did *not* tamper with were the holy words of the living God. The purity of these words of God were agreed upon by the scholars in Israel and settled books of scripture were in common use in the

---

3) *Did Jesus Use the Septuagint?* (Chick Publications, 2017) www.chick.com.

synagogues. Throughout this early history, God's protection of His words makes it clear that God's agenda was to *preserve* His words for all future generations. That's why David was inspired to write these words:

> Psalms 12:6-7: "The words of the LORD are pure words: as silver tried in a furnace of earth, purified seven times. *Thou shalt keep them, O LORD, thou shalt preserve them from this generation for ever.*"

God told Moses to entrust the teaching and passing down of the scriptures to the Levites. In addition, every father in his family was responsible for passing down the words of God, even writing them on the doorposts of his house!

> Deuteronomy 6:6-9: "And these words, which I command thee this day, shall be in thine heart: And thou shalt teach them diligently unto thy children, and shalt talk of them when thou sittest in thine house, and when thou walkest by the way, and when thou liest down, and when thou risest up. And thou shalt bind them for a sign upon thine hand, and they shall be as frontlets between thine eyes. And thou shalt write them upon the posts of thy house, and on thy gates."

These were *very* literate people.

And who were the big interpreters of the Bible in Jesus' day? God called them the *scribes*. Scribes are writers by definition, but these were also trained lawyers, the intellectuals (scholars) among the literate.

Chapter 3

Jesus The Master Scholar

I wish I could have been a bug on the wall.

At just 12 years of age, Jesus' *questions* astounded the intellectuals of Israel, who spent their time debating at the south wing of the temple in Jerusalem:

> Luke 2:46-47: "And it came to pass, that after three days they found him in the temple, sitting in the midst of the doctors, both hearing them, and *asking them questions.* And all that heard him were astonished at *his understanding and answers."*

This happened around the time of His bar mitzvah, and already the people couldn't match His intellect. Of course, He happened to be God. But that didn't stop Him also being a scholar.

During the ministry of Jesus, we see the tit-for-tat between Jesus, promoting God's agenda, and the scholars with their self-serving agenda. Of course, He had an edge, being their Creator. Nevertheless, He proved that the best scholarship of the Devil's academics was way off base with their perverse agenda. They couldn't catch up to Jesus' thinking with a spaceship.

JESUS THE MASTER SCHOLAR

Jesus always asked questions the scholars could not answer

Throughout His ministry, Jesus exposed their agenda: they ran a political machine, rather than being concerned for the truth. However, before He left, He issued an iron-clad promise: "Heaven and earth shall pass away, but my words shall not pass away." (Matt. 24.35; Mark 13:31; Luke 21:33)

Chapter 4

New Testament Scholars

Luke, the Beloved Scholar

Most people think of Luke as the "beloved physician" (Colossian 4:14). But they often forget he was a scholar. Just like John, Luke wrote about specific people, places and events that only an eyewitness could have known. But he also properly used nautical, political, chronological and social terms, exactly as the people in those trades knew them. He wasn't writing as a man on the periphery. He was writing as a scholar. And as I hinted, just in his two books, Luke and Acts, he wrote more words than Paul did in all of his epistles —even if you include Hebrews!

John the Secret Scholar

I remember nights at the library at Bible college, reading liberal Bible commentators. They exalted their own ideas and quoted one another's theories. But for at least two centuries, these anti-biblical scholars have repeatedly said "John was no scholar." Greek teachers pointed out that his use of Greek was simpler than that of other New Testament writers. After a while, they decided it wasn't John at all, but a church committee writing in the 2nd century, far removed from the events.

I read about it in Bible college. Then I met professors who believed it when I was at Fuller Seminary.

But the 20th century revealed some amazing things. Archaeologists, utilizing the words that John penned, were able to figure out the locations of the two pools John mentioned, the one at the sheep gate and the other, the pool of Bethesda. But there is no way anyone could know about those places after the destruction of Jerusalem in AD 70, much less after about 120 AD, when the entire area was cemented over.

Someone had to know where the high priest's house was, and locations of other important buildings. Only a person ***alive at the exact time*** these events took place could know facts like these.

The scriptures give us another hint: John 18:15: "*And Simon Peter followed Jesus, and so did another disciple: **that disciple was known unto the high priest**, and went in with Jesus into the palace of the high priest.*"

I think John was a Levite. He "was known" by the high priest, which is no small feat. He lived in Capernaum. How would he have distinguished himself to the highest official in Jerusalem? (That is a story we can ask him about when we get to heaven.) But it gave John easy access to his house! Wow! Try that with your governor or favorite TV preacher and see how far you get.

Paul The Prolific Scholar

When we think of the New Testament, let's be honest. We think of the apostle Paul. The modern scholars do, for sure. He wrote more ***books*** than any other author, in the form of letters or epistles. But he didn't write more ***words***. That honor goes to Luke.

After the resurrection, Jesus chose Paul, one of the top scholars in Israel to expand His kingdom to the Gentiles. Trained by the best Hebrew scholars of his day, he majored in the Hebrew "Bible," our Old Testament.

God chose Paul to take the disciples' written accounts of Jesus' words and create a systematic, comprehensive, scholarly presentation of the gospel. He started with the Old Testament scriptures and led the listener to salvation by faith in Christ, rather than obedience to the law of Moses. Yet throughout his life, Paul fought a running battle with the Judaizers, who claimed that their scholars required that the Gentiles obey the entire Jewish law in order to be saved.

Chapter 5

Early Church Fathers

Many people are confused about who the church fathers were. People usually refer to the ones starting about 100+ AD. They are divided by the time in which they spoke, and the language they wrote, Latin or Greek. But the true early church fathers are just eight people: Matthew, Mark, Luke, John, Peter, Paul, James and Jude.

These were the only "fathers" to the church. They were inspired by the holy Spirit of God. Everything they wrote is doctrine we can rely on. No one else comes close.

In comparison, everyone else is a pretender to the title. Every other writer ***wrote without being inspired of God.*** Every other one ***wrote his own opinions, not God's words.*** And we can take them or leave them. But the eight *actual* church fathers, we must trust with our hearts, because they wrote exactly what **God** wanted them to. No one else after them can claim that level of inspiration.

This is key: every book of the "church fathers" (or in theologian-speak, the patristics) involves writings that are uninspired and tainted either less or more. No one had it all right. That's what happens when humans write without God's Holy Ghost moving them.

"For the prophecy came not in old time by the will of man: but

holy men of God spake as they were moved by the Holy Ghost." (2 Peter 1:21)

The Holy Ghost moved the New Testament scholars, the **real** church fathers. His wind drove their sails. The others were puffing into the sails of their boats.

Why is this?

The patristic scholars are unreliable. And many were instrumental in creating the prostitute church that developed in the Vatican in Rome. Here are some examples:

Origen taught two opposing doctrines, depending upon whether the student was one of his elect, or not.

200-253 AD - Two-faced **Origen** taught "orthodoxy" publicly to some students, and esoteric occultic religion, at the same time, to special, "elect" pupils.

Created the Hexapla through many servants —a bunch of versions, with his own version and notes as well.

October 312-337 - Politician and Emperor **Constantine** maneuvered himself into being "bishop of bishops" and the first pope. He also convened "church" councils to determine what doctrines would be accepted in his "Christianized" empire.

380s-405 - Stuck-up scholar **Jerome** made his own Catholic Latin version of the Greek and Hebrew Bible books and added apocryphal books he translated from various languages.

Aug 24, 410 - **Visigoths** invaded Rome. After Rome fell, the Bishop of Rome collected properties, making this counterfeit church the most powerful entity, both religious and political.

During this period, Church Councils met to resolve questions that arose about various doctrines:

Council	Date	Purpose
First Ecumenical Council (Nicea)	325	Doctrine of Christ's divinity; Easter made to never be the same as Passover
2nd Ecumenical Council (Constantinople)	381	Doctrine of the Trinity
3rd Ecumenical Council (Ephesus)	431	Mary defined as bearer of God (*theotokos*). This was the official beginning of Catholic Mary being called "the mother of God."
4th Ecumenical Council (Chalcedon)	451	Jesus defined as 100% God, 100% man

Some things the committees decided were scriptural. Others were not. The moral of the story is we don't need councils. We need scripture. We need to trust scripture. So, we need to have scripture we can trust.

Modern church scholars have come up with different groupings of these "church fathers":
- Apostolic
- Post-apostolic
- Ante-Nicene (Before the council of Nicea in 325.)
- Nicene

- Post-Nicene (After the council of Nicea.)

And they were grouped another way by language:
- Greek Fathers
- Latin Fathers

These guys are all a mixed bag. Soon after the apostles died, some began venerating dead people. Christians who died for their faith would have their graves visited by other Christians, who lifted them up above the rest of them.

One story of this quasi-worship given to dead people involves Origen, who, as a teen, tried to run and die with the martyrs one day when his dad, Leonidas, was being led away to be beheaded for his faith. His mother held him back only by hiding his clothes. His sense of modesty, at least, overrode his passion for following other Christians to their death.

Origen became one of the most prominent "fathers" in the modern text critic's history of the Bible. Origen's own Greek Septuagint, the 5th column of his giant parallel Old Testament called the "Hexapla," became the main version of the Septuagint Old Testament that circulated from that day forward in the proto-Catholic churches.[4]

Why is Origen important? He was an *extremist* in just about every sense of the word. Like Freemasonry, he taught both *exoteric* doctrines (the religion seen by the public) and *esoteric* (secret doctrines for the "initiated" or "elect").

The codices [CO dih sees], "big books," that are labeled as "Alexandrian," are known as Sinaiticus, Vaticanus, and Alexandrinus. Nowadays those are the Greek Bibles that scholars connect to Origen and what they consider *his* Septuagint.

Origen has continued to be revered by Catholics, text critics, Protestants and even occultists. We must be careful

---

4) *Did Jesus Use the Septuagint?* (Chick Publications, 2017)

when examining his writings. He is a truly mixed bag. He was honest in one regard: his work on the Hexapla did at least use symbols to note which words were translated from the Hebrew, and which were not.

Chapter 6

Two Types of Scholars; Two Agendas

At this point it is useful to look at the progress of the doubting scholars, who had not been idle. As the gospel spread, the multiplication of local churches led to groupings we now call sects, or later *denominations,* when they tried to adhere to truth, and known as *cults* if they did not.

How they handled the words of God determined which category they fit into. Those who cherished pure scriptures that they could trust, came under heavy attack by those who wished to pollute the Bible to create doubt.

For example, two versions of the Old Testament emerged. One was faithful to the carefully preserved Hebrew manuscripts. It was preserved by the descendants of the Levitical priests, called the Masoretes, and it became known as Masoretic Text. The other, the Septuagint, inserted the Apocrypha folk tales to support unbiblical teachings.

Some of the early scholars who were determined to protect the pure scriptures include Valentinus (AD 100-160), and translators of the Old Latin (ca AD 157) and Syrian (AD 150). Portions were translated into Anglo-Saxon by the Venerable Bede (died in 735), and King Alfred (849-899). Later, Wycliffe, Erasmus, Luther and Tyndale picked up the torch toward a preserved English Bible.[5] Their works, along with those of John Rogers, Myles Coverdale and Theodore Beza, formed the basis for the King James Bible.

Starting with John Wycliffe, godly scholars sought to translate the words of God faithfully into English.

In the company of the doubters were men like Clement of Alexandria (150-215), Origen (184-253), Eusebius (265-340), Augustine (354-430), and Jerome (347-420). After about 500 AD the counterfeit church (Roman Catholicism) switched from debates between scholars to blunt force against the true church. When found, their Bibles were simply piled up and burned. By the 600s they began to torch Bible believers at the stake, as well.

There are two different changes that occurred when the last apostle passed away, around 100 AD. The Bible-believers needed their Bible. The Christians wanted the writings of these apostles and God-approved, inspired writers, to be collected together. So God helped this to happen in Antioch of Syria.

But the Devil was hard at work from this point in time as well, developing cults that adapted the Bible to the Greek and

---

5) See "The Translators Revived" by Alexander McClure and *Did the Catholic Church Give Us the Bible?* (Chick Publications, 2005) chapters 4-5.

other mystery religions, philosophies and cults. They ***changed Bible texts*** to suit their masters, their cult gurus. Then they spread them as fast as they could, even though they contradicted each other. This was the *first* change.

Dean Burgon quoted Caius (Gaius the presbyter), who lived and wrote close to 200 AD:

> "The Divine Scriptures," he says, "these heretics have audaciously corrupted: …. laying violent hands upon them under pretense of correcting them. That I bring no false accusation, any one who is disposed may easily convince himself. He has but to collect the copies belonging to these persons severally; then, to compare one with another; and he will discover that their discrepancy is extraordinary.
>
> "Those of Asclepiades, at all events, will be found discordant from those of Theodotus. Now, plenty of specimens of either sort are obtainable, inasmuch as these men's disciples have industriously multiplied the (so-called) 'corrected' copies of their respective teachers, which are in reality nothing else but 'corrupted' copies. With the foregoing copies again, those of Hemophilus will be found entirely at variance.
>
> "As for the copies of Apollonides, they even contradict one another. Nay, let any one compare the fabricated text which these persons put forth in the first instance, with that which exhibits their latest perversions of the Truth, and he will discover that the disagreement between them is even excessive.
>
> "Of the enormity of the offence of which these men

have been guilty, they must needs themselves be fully aware. Either they do not believe that the Divine Scriptures are the utterance of the Holy Ghost, in which case they are to be regarded as unbelievers: or else, they account themselves wiser than the Holy Ghost,—and what is that, but to have the faith of devils? As for their denying their guilt, the thing is impossible, seeing that the copies under discussion are their own actual handywork ...."[6]

With God only listing **elders**, **pastors**, and **teachers** in the New Testament, there was not room for a power structure. Those who led had the heart of a servant. They were *servant-leaders.*

"And whosoever will be chief among you, let him be your servant:" Matthew 20:27

But starting about 100 AD, there were political and social changes, as well. People in groups always want to know who is the greatest.

"At the same time came the disciples unto Jesus, saying, Who is the greatest in the kingdom of heaven?" Matthew 18:1

"And there was also a strife among them, which of them should be accounted the greatest." Luke 22:24

The early Christian churches did the same. They ended up copying the Roman hierarchical system of government, substituting church names for the Roman offices. Then they made up other offices for the church. That put some ministers above others, and others above them. And that ***hierarchical structure*** became the ground work for the counterfeit "church," the Whore of Babylon, the Roman Catholic papacy. That was the *second* change.

---

6) Quoted in Dean Burgon, *The Revision Revised* (1881), pp. 323-324.

Do we trust the church leaders who wrote after the apostles and other inspired scripture writers? We must carefully evaluate all these writings. But what are our criteria? Some of the church leaders trusted the scriptures. Others came up with their own ideas.

Those agendas are not equal.

Scholars who wrote the scriptures cannot be equal with scholars who were not inspired by God. One must be dominant. So before anything else, you have to ask yourself a simple question:

Which scholars do I trust?

If your faith is in the revealed words of God in scripture, then the scripture-writing scholars win. If your faith is in a favorite post-biblical interpreter, then the uninspired scholars win.

The scripture-writing scholars were followed by Bible believers who collected and faithfully translated and spread those words. That became a stream of scriptures that we call **the pure stream**, because these believers were committed to making exact copies and word-for-word translations. This stream had its head in Antioch.

"…And the disciples were called Christians first in Antioch." Acts 11:26

The doubting scholars, who questioned scriptures and valued their theological, philosophical and other training and beliefs over the Bible, reinterpreted the scripture and progressively changed it to suit their lack of faith in what God said. Their writings, as disjointed and varied as they are, became a second stream of scriptures that we call **the polluted stream**.[7]

---

7) See *Did the Catholic Church Give Us the Bible?* (Chick Publications, 2005), chapter 2, on the two streams of manuscripts.

TWO TYPES OF SCHOLARS; TWO AGENDAS

The spigot of this filth was located in Alexandria, Egypt, the same place where they formed the Septuagint in the first century AD,[8] and kept modifying it into the 200s and 300s.

The doubting scholars met at the Museum of Alexandria. Ancient museums weren't showcases of dead things. They were gathering places for philosophers and theologians and inventors to share their ideas, to "muse" together.

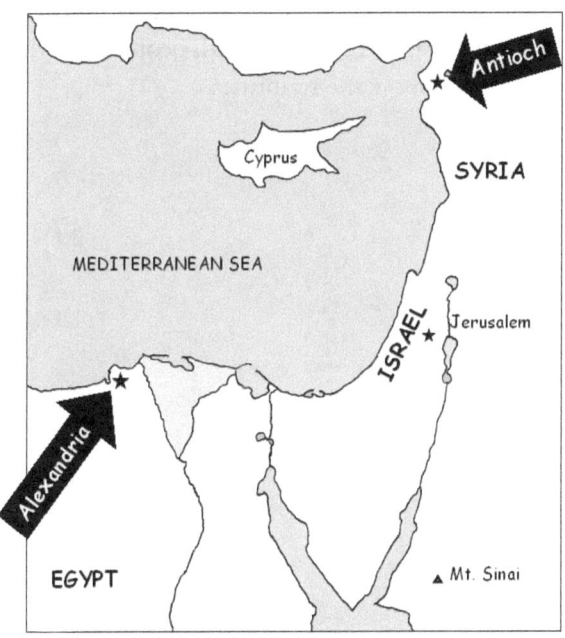

The two centers for Bible texts: Antioch of Syria for the preserved, and Alexandria, Egypt for the polluted.

Picture this: one group of scholars, originating up north of Israel in Antioch of Syria, was dedicated to faithfully passing on the exact words and exact meaning of scriptures, in

---

8) *Did Jesus Use the Septuagint?* (Chick Publications, 2017)

whatever language. Another group, southwest in Alexandria, Egypt, had an agenda to push their own philosophical and religious beliefs. They used their polluted Bibles as a cover to steer people away from faith in the preserved Bible to having faith in themselves.

So even though the doubting scholars claimed to hold to Christianity as a belief system, they didn't submit to scripture. They attempted to make scripture submit to **them.** Many of these people were more concerned with people following *them*, than for *them* to follow the scriptures.

CHAPTER 7

EARLY CHURCH SCHOLARS

After Paul, two streams of manuscripts were produced by scholars with two different agendas. As detailed in ***Did the Catholic Church Give Us the Bible?,*** the stream from Antioch in Syria flowed out through Asia Minor into Europe and became the fountainhead for the Bibles of the Reformation, 1300 years later.

The scholars in this stream believed Jesus' promise to *preserve* His words and that they were dealing with *the very words of God.* They saw their task as to make exact copies and faithful translations into the languages needed, so they could obey the Great Commission and take the gospel to "all nations."

The other stream can be traced from Alexandria, Egypt, ultimately across the Mediterranean to the Vatican. The agenda of the scholars in this stream differed from the northern stream. To them, the Hebrew scriptures were just another competing system of philosophy and theology along with the other schools of thought of the day.

Their manuscripts, as produced in pure Egyptian form, showed that they did not believe that Jesus was eternally God or that there was anything unique about the Hebrew writings. To these Egyptian philosophers, it was no more valid a system than the systems of other cultures. Today this is called *cultural relativity.*

By about 150 in the Antioch stream, the Bible had been translated into Syrian, also called Aramaic, since "Aram" in the Old Testament is the same as "Syria" in Greek. And no later than 157 AD, the Bible had been translated into what we call Old Latin; By 200 AD copies were said to be in the British Isles.

There is something we must always keep in mind. Every one of these copies was hand-made, one at a time. Let no professor deceive you. There were no copy machines. There were no printing presses. There was no mass production. So how good a copy was made depended upon the dedication and faith of the copyist.

Greek, Old Latin, Aramaic and other copies and translations that originated from the Antiochian stream, untainted by the philosophies and cults of Egypt and Greece, were part of the heritage of the pure stream that led to the King James Bible.

But Satan was also preparing a counterfeit church to ***distract*** from the real one. As soon as the Roman government began to crumble, the Caesars changed their robes and baptized their pagan system of idolatry labeling it "Christian."[9]

Today that counterfeit church is known as Roman Catholicism. It has progressively taken on the exact characteristics of the prostitute "church" in Revelation chapters 17 and 18.[10] The Catholic scholar Jerome was tasked with creating a Bible

---

9) See *Did the Catholic Church Give Us the Bible?* (Chick Publications, 2005), Chapter 3.
10) See *Why They Changed the Bible* (Chick Publications, 2014), Chapter 16.

that would support, or at least not contradict, their burgeoning worship of the wafer god and Virgin Mary goddess.

Jerome's changes included a different gender of a single word in Genesis 3:15. "And I will put enmity between thee and the woman, and between thy seed and her seed: **she** (the woman, instead of **it** her seed,) shall bruise thy head, and thou shalt bruise his heel."

This change in Jerome's Latin Bible of 405 AD was carried over into the 1610 Douay-Rheims English version and was *not corrected* until the publication of the New American Bible... **in 1970**.[11] During those 1,565 years, thousands of statues and icons were made showing the Virgin Mary goddess with her foot on a serpent.[12] And statues, icons, drawings and paintings are *still* made with Mary's foot on a snake to this very day. And it came from the change of gender of a single pronoun.

Where changes were not feasible, the Catholic system simply reinterpreted the scripture. For example: support for the worship of the Eucharist comes from a distorted interpretation of Christ's message of "the bread of life" in John chapter 6. The justification for the office of the pope comes from a misreading of Matt. 16:18-19, Christ's statement to Peter, whom they claim to be the first pope.

Taking selections from the Alexandrian stream of manuscripts, the scholars of this counterfeit church created a series of Roman Catholic Bibles, first in Greek, then in Latin, and necessarily included the Apocrypha to justify some of their pagan-based doctrines.

But scholarly leaders in the northern stream, such as Ignatius

---

11) The change to the Latin Nova Vulgata (New Vulgate) did not occur until 1979.
12) See *Did Jesus Use the Septuagint?* (Chick Publications, 2017), pages 88-89.

of Antioch (died 108 AD) and Polycarp of Smyrna (martyred in 155 AD by the Romans), began quoting scriptures in their writings, revealing which ones were universally accepted as inspired.

Copies of translations which we have in Syriac and Old Latin from before the 200s AD show a settled consensus of an accepted canon of scripture. Bible believers compiled our present New Testament during this period.

Looking back from the perspective of those who believe God preserved His words, it was God's guidance of believers, not the majority vote of a committee or council, that selected the books for His Bible.

The New Testament that emerged as the finished book was combined with a faithful copy of the Hebrew Bible, our Old Testament, to become the sources of our present Protestant Bible.

Since the commercial language (or "trade language") of the world of Jesus' day was Greek, the Greek text became the foundational document for copies and translations as the northern stream expanded into Europe, Africa, and Great Britain.

The details of the medieval history of that stream are not very clear, primarily because of the extreme persecution of the people who had those texts. Groups like the Vaudois (and later Waldenses), the Albigenses, and the Anabaptists made careful hand copies but when found, they were often burned.

In one record that we do have, a whole library was discovered and torched by the enemies of the gospel.[13] The popes

---

13) See Luigi DeSanctis, *Popery, Puseyism, Jesuitism: Described in a Series of Letters*, p. 53; General History of the Evangelical Churches of the Piedmont Valleys by Jean Leger, 1669.

were quite effective in pulling the levers of political power, driving the true Bible believers into hiding.

We do know that the gospel spread quickly after the church was scattered from Jerusalem. One record places Latin Bibles In England as early as 200 AD.

One helpful small source, from a Baptist perspective, of details of the persecution of the true scholars during the dark ages is *The Trail of Blood*, by Dr. J. M. Carroll (1931). Copies are available from several sources on the internet.

> Carroll sums it up thus: During every period of the "Dark Ages" there were in existence many Christians and many separate and independent Churches, some of them dating back to the times of the Apostles, which were never in any way connected with the Catholic Church. They always wholly rejected and repudiated the Catholics and their pagan-based doctrines. This is a fact clearly demonstrated by credible history.
>
> These Christians were the perpetual objects of bitter and relentless persecution. History shows that during the period of the "Dark Ages," about twelve centuries, beginning with A.D. 426, there were about fifty millions of these Christians who died martyr deaths. Very many thousands of others, both preceding and succeeding the "Dark Ages," died under the same hard hand of persecution.

After centuries of inquisitions, extermination of Christians almost became a spectator sport, as it had been at Rome.

Throughout this process, the scholars of the counterfeit church were busy promoting its Bibles that were polluted with the unscriptural Apocrypha, supporting their increasingly pagan-based idol worship. ***Did the Catholic Church Give Us the Bible?*** provides additional details of this period.

CHAPTER 8

WARFARE AGAINST THE "GOOD GUY" SCHOLARS

Satan always plays rough if he can get away with it. The doubting Catholic scholars hooked up with the emerging national governments, prodding them to use its police power to eliminate the promoters of the pure line of scriptures. This period includes the infamous Inquisitions, starting in Toulouse, France in 1220, setting the torch to thousands of Bibles and millions of Bible believers.

The power behind these attacks was centered in the counterfeit church headquartered in Rome. But when murderous persecution failed to eliminate the pure scriptures, Satan began to execute a subtle plan "B." Since lies are always his primary tool, he began concocting a false history to fight the true history.

COUNTERFEITING AS WARFARE

Since counterfeiting is one of the Devil's favorite tools, he used the counterfeit church to enlist doubting scholars to create corrupted Bibles that look very much like the real thing. Satan was attempting to eliminate the world-wide effectiveness of the pure words of God.

Old Latin

When the Gospel spread west from Antioch in Syria, one of the early translations was in Latin, known today as "Old Latin." It was called the Latin Vulgate, meaning for the common man. This became a foundation document for the later scholars who used it, with others, to create the stream of English translations.

Catholic Latin Vulgate

But the scholars of the doubting stream created their own polluted Latin Bible, again containing the Apocrypha, that they also called "The" Latin Vulgate. These two different "Vulgates" have caused some confusion with more modern scholars. We will see later the effectiveness of Satan's use of counterfeiting.

The Devil hated and still hates the words of God. If someone has God's words, he or she can grow in faith.

"So then faith cometh by hearing, and hearing by the word of God." Romans 10:17

Satan did all he could to destroy those words, and pervert as many as he could. But he didn't get away with much. When the time was right, God simply had His scholars assemble the right texts into one Bible. That product would be God's preserved words, first in Hebrew, next in Greek, and then in English.

In the simplest of terms, those who have the biggest army are the ones who write the history. When Rome's Caesars changed their robes for the garb of "holy Roman" popes, they quickly moved to suppress all who disagreed with their way of doing things. Over the centuries, persecutions of true Christians accelerated, and Bible believers' writings were confiscated and destroyed.

There are not a lot of writings by these persecuted Christians left today. The Devil was successful in destroying most, but not all, of their writings. Roman Catholics only wrote *very* biased histories about them, justifying their persecution. And yet, when we read the writings of faithful Christians who knew these martyrs, we can see they accepted them as brothers and sisters in Christ. This is why, in the 20th century, some Christians have called this almost silent history "the trail of blood."

We can put together the testimonies of Bible believing Christians whose writings survived and compare them to the hateful writings against them by the Roman Catholics. And from that combination a picture emerges of who these people were. And though we do not have at hand all their own writings, we can put together what they believed by reading these testimonies, both of their friends and of their enemies.

This is key: when a Roman Catholic persecutor compared any particular person or group to the modern Reformation, we then know much about their beliefs, as well as what kind of Bible they had. For instance, Martin Luther had the Tepl translation at hand as he created his German Bible. The Tepl was an older German Bible, translated from Old Latin texts in the pure line.

From time to time evidence emerges from the Middle Ages, that testifies to the agenda of the scholars who held to the pure line of scripture. The doctrines they held also bore witness to which line of scripture they trusted, as well as which "church fathers" and other scholars they rejected.

But what's the final proof of the pudding? The results. The *fruit*. The fruit of the English Bible of 1611 is a powerful, active *faith* in the people who read and believe its words. That is why it birthed the world's largest missionary movement and multiple revivals since it was published. The fruit of the Roman Catholic Vulgate and even more in the modern Greek texts, however, has been *doubt* in even the most basic doctrines about the Godhead, Christ, salvation, faith vs. works and the nature of eternity.

And only one line has been fought against, tooth and nail by the Devil and his minions, as well as the false scholars with their agendas.

I'm sure you know which stream it is.

CHAPTER 9

TRUTH EXPLODES

While Satan was realigning his strategy of doubt, trust in the truth was exploding.

Erasmus' text laid the groundwork for a century of developing the English and other Reformation Bibles.

Starting in 1516, Desiderius Erasmus prepared faithful Latin and Greek scriptures, followed up by scholars such as Robert Estienne and Theodore Beza. They, in turn, were utilized by English scholars such as William Tyndale, John Rogers, Myles Coverdale, and many other scholars who fled to Geneva.

These scholars, who believed that God preserved His words, were determined to free the scriptures from obscure languages known only to the few who were learned and give even unschooled plowboys access to the pure words of God.

God set all this up at the perfect time in history. Up to a

few decades earlier, people had to make their Bibles by hand. But in the mid-1400s, Johann Gutenberg combined moveable type with the newly developed inexpensive paper. And once this new technology spread, "great was the company of those that published" God's word!

Gutenberg's press was part of God's plan to bring His words in multiple identical copies to the world.

Once people began to read for themselves what God said, they realized (as did Martin Luther) that the Roman Catholic system was a counterfeit of what God called His church in the scriptures. The Catholic religion wasn't Christ's bride —it was a prostitute! This realization resulted in the great spiritual move known as the Reformation. Over the next decades, the Lord cemented the preserved Bible text into millions of identical printed copies for world-wide dissemination. These pure texts of the scriptures became the solid foundation for worldwide revivals and missionary efforts. And the proof of its root was its fruit: an explosion of faith, in God and His words.

The Jesuits under Rome redoubled their efforts, and over the decades, many nations fell back under the sway of the pope. But England was another story. God helped England to succeed where others failed, providing even miracles. Even the king of Spain admitted his great Spanish Armada was destroyed, not by English might, but by the wind! And England succeeded in repelling the persecutions and outright warfare, both openly by Vatican-backed armies, and in secret by Jesuit spies. All this allowed time for a beachhead to be established in America, for the promotion of the trusted scriptures.

In the 400 years since then, we have seen major progress toward fulfilling Matt. 24:14 that the gospel would be "preached in all the world for a witness unto all nations; and then shall the end come."

If we take a closer look at the history just described, good scholars and bad scholars have been deeply embedded in the process. In short, the good scholars fought for purity of copies and translations of copies. But the scholars who fell under the weight of the diabolical agenda, wound up creating doubt in God's words.

I've already referenced one legion of foot soldiers of the counterfeit church. It was started in 1540 by Ignatius of Loyola, and known as the Society of Jesus, or *the Jesuit order*. It utilized its brainwashed army to mount a sophisticated Counter-Reformation, to undo all the progress of the truth. Its priests, called Jesuits, became advanced scholars, both intellectually and politically. They used the confessional to discover political secrets, and education to condition the youth. They became "confessors of the powerful and teachers of their children." And so they are to this day.

Chapter 10

The Counter-Reformation: A New Kind of Attack

Satan's fiery Inquisition, fed by the Council of Trent (1545-63), failed to eliminate all the Bibles and Bible-believers. Because of these simple, faithful men and women, others were encouraged to stand and spread the words of God. So, the Devil turned to the scholarly community with greater force. The Jesuits immediately set to make a counterfeit Bible that looked like Tyndale's but was just a recycled Catholic Vulgate. The Catholic Latin Vulgate had never caught any traction among the general public. Only priests were allowed to have them. And all translations of the Bible in a common language were forbidden. So, in 1610 the Rheims-Douay was unleashed.

"...out of many good ones, one principal good one, not justly to be excepted against..." (from the 1611 KJV preface, From the Translators to the Reader)

THE COUNTER-REFORMATION: A NEW KIND OF ATTACK

Meanwhile, the venerable English Bible of 1611, authorized by King James VI of Scotland and I of England soon became the world standard. Translations of it were spread to dozens of other languages and nations.

"Update" the Bible

Satan hatched his next plot in the colleges and universities, from France to Germany to England. Finally, Satan got a break by the 1800s when doubting scholars started to propose that King James's 200-year-old classic English Version needed "updating." Believing scholars warned that it would be a dangerous opportunity for the doubting scholars to start changing the text. But Satan's "enlightened" were in place. The doubters charged ahead with their plans.

Bible Societies were quickly formed and soon both Catholics and unbelieving scholars were invited to have a say in how the societies functioned. See *Why They Changed the Bible,* starting at page 164, for further intriguing details.

Since it didn't work to simply switch Bibles, the doubting scholars came upon another strategy: they claimed they wanted to "fix" the "errors" in the King James! But they didn't appeal to the preserved Greek for this "fix." Instead, they secretly switched the texts, substituting the scissors-and-paste Bible using the fraudulent Vaticanus and Sinaiticus Greek texts, approved by Rome.

Once this was achieved, in the English Revised Version of 1881-85 and the American Standard of 1901, the doubters switched their focus to changing crucial words, watering down the Bible so it would be more compatible with what would become the future one-world religion.

Preservation Doctrine Attacked

Honest scholars had from the beginning believed that Jesus meant it when He said, "Heaven and earth shall pass away, but my words shall not pass away." (Matt. 24:35)

The engineers of doubt had to derail that notion.

That was a lot of history in a few words. Let me give you a bit more detail.

In 1804 the British and Foreign Bible Society (BFBS) was formed to get Bibles out. They promised to use the King James text, without note or comment, and with no Apocryphal books. However, they were compromised from the start. For years, donors' money went to Bibles with the Apocrypha, and to Catholics who made their own Bibles to spread.

What's more, they included Unitarians, who denied Jesus was eternally God, and banned prayer in Jesus' name! Eventually one group that left in disgust formed the Trinitarian Bible Society and made King James Bibles. The BFBS, on the other hand, became ripe for the next move: revision of the Bible. The newly made American Bible Society slowly followed suit.

The revisers, who were Bible-doubting scholars, were determined to carry out their scheme. By 1852 two Cambridge professors, Brooke Foss Westcott and Fenton John Anthony Hort, decided to change the Greek text. By 1870 they figured that their best course was to claim to "update" the Authorized Bible. The Church of England had two Convocations to convince. The northern Convocation in York stood opposed to the idea. But the southern Convocation of Canterbury gave a limited go-ahead. The revisers were presented guidelines, which history shows they largely ignored.

THE COUNTER-REFORMATION: A NEW KIND OF ATTACK

B.F. Westcott and F.J.A. Hort paved the way for all new Bibles with their "Westcott-Hort theory" that has never been fully abandoned by doubting scholars.

It seems Westcott and Hort wanted Bible-doubters of all kinds. Just like the British and Foreign Bible Society, Westcott and several of his select disciples decided there needed to be Unitarians, who denied the eternal Godhood of Jesus, in the Revision Committee. They even tried to get turncoat-to-Catholicism John Newman on the Committee, but he declined.

Only one text critic was clearly inclined toward the preserved text, F.H.A. Scrivener. With this hand-picked group, the Bible-doubting scholars held sway. And in 1881, the English Revised Version New Testament (the ERV) was foisted upon an unsuspecting world as the first "Revised King James."

ERV: First Doubting Bible

This ERV was based on a secretly-switched Greek text. God's words were largely changed to match a "critical text." That "critical text" tried to make sense of the inconsistent readings of two supposedly ancient Greek codices (big books): Codex Sinaiticus and Codex Vaticanus. Sinaiticus had only been published in 1862, 8 years before the Revision began. And the accepted form of the Vaticanus was only published in

1867, less than 3 years before the revisers met. Both editions were made by a Bible-doubter named Constantin Tischendorf.

By claiming these giant Greek Bibles were "older and better," and denying the common people permission to see them for themselves, a giant disinformation campaign was launched to replace the Authorized Bible with whatever their scholars said was an "older and better" reading —even if it removed some verses and made others contradict each other. Then they took the focus off the thousands of manuscripts that agreed with each other to get their congregations to stop trusting their Bible.

Fake History

They concocted a story that is still told today: that "because the Sinaiticus and Vaticanus were older, they must be more accurate to the originals." Therefore, where the King James readings differed, they claimed those parts "must have been added later."

Then in 1882, Westcott and Hort made up a fake history out of whole cloth. Without any evidence whatsoever, they claimed that there must have been a huge meeting of church leaders around the 300s A.D. At this meeting they supposedly decided on which Bible text they liked: the one with lots of added words they were used to using.

They decided they didn't want the "more accurate" Alexandrian text and got to work copying this augmented Bible as their accepted book. Then they went back to their churches, all over the ancient world. This theory claimed that the "more accurate" Alexandrian Bibles got relegated to a desert graveyard. That is why, they say, the Alexandrian Bibles were found in the desert, and why now upwards of 5,700 Bible

THE COUNTER-REFORMATION: A NEW KIND OF ATTACK

manuscripts are pretty much the same, though each one was hand copied.

This theory adds in one more claim, that Vaticanus and Sinaiticus are somehow two of the Bibles that were more accurate, and thus rejected by this imaginary 300s AD committee. They placed more trust in Bible verses where Vaticanus and Sinaiticus agreed, than on the history of the vast majority of Bible manuscripts.

Because of this, in 1881 they produced the new English Revised Version translation (ERV) of the New Testament based primarily on the Sinaiticus and Vaticanus documents. However, the revisers didn't change and remove as much as Westcott and Hort's Greek text did. Some of the words their made-up text removed were so offensive, that even the revisers themselves preferred to keep the traditional words in their Bible, despite Westcott's pleading and pouting.

Now let me tell you a bit of history about two different kinds of marginal notes.

In the 1611 King James translation process, the over 50 translators agreed to a rule. If after the 14 or so times they went over the text, some scholar still held to a certain word or phrase, they wrote it into the margin, preceded by the word "Or." That is why I say about King James marginal notes, "If it says 'or,' you can ignore." The text of the King James is what all or almost all the translators agreed upon —an amazing achievement of both English literature and Bible translation, that stands to this day. We focus on the **text** of the King James, not the marginal notes.

So, the marginal notes were not a detriment to faith.

That all changed, starting with the ERV. Some of their clever marginal notes actually changed entire doctrines by switching a couple of words. Other notes cast doubt upon entire phrases or verses. At times they wrote a heretical doctrine into the text (like 2 Timothy 3:16 in the ERV), sometimes with the original words in the footnotes. These marginal notes, in contrast to the King James, led readers into a swamp of doubt. They also opened the door for endless debate (and endless revisions) by later generations of doubting textual scholars.

But Christ's guarantee that He would preserve His words still hung like a frown over their rebellion. Two professors from Princeton University attempted to alleviate their guilt. They figured, if the doctrine says "preservation," then change the doctrine! A. A. Hodges and B. B. Warfield proposed a change to the Westminster Confession, in the doctrine of preservation of scriptures, that did exactly that.

Preservation Doctrine Replaced by OAO

Their new doctrine, that I call Original Autographs Only (OAO), asserted that only the original autographs *were* truly inerrant (without error). But alas! No original autographs exist today. On top of that, all copies made by those originals have errors, too! I have no idea how they can prove that, since they don't have the originals to compare them to. But that didn't stop them.

The OAO doctrine has been taught from April of 1881, four months before the ERV was released, to the present day. What started in Princeton University is now in the statements of faith in conservative Christian churches and taught in Bible colleges and seminaries. Maybe even yours.

According to OAO, all subsequent documents contained intentional or accidental errors left by sloppy copyists or translators with their own ideas.[14] That means it's now up to the *scholars* to decide which readings they feel are *most likely* to be what God said. When they can't agree, which is often, they simply add a footnote and push the decision off to the reader, as to which one *he* or *she* likes. This essentially leaves us with a multiple-choice Bible, up for grabs as to what God really said.

It became popular and "scholarly" to ignore Christ's promise to preserve His words. This divided scholars into two camps. In one camp were the world-class scholars with a godly agenda, who labored for nearly 6 years to produce a faithful Bible in English from excellent representatives of carefully guarded manuscripts.

Real NT Lost "Forever"?

On the other hand, we had (and still have) scholars who have endlessly debated about what they think God really said (or meant to say) and have concluded that we cannot really know. In fact, one of those scholars, Frederick Cornwallis Conybeare (1856-1924) flatly stated "…the ultimate [New Testament] text, if there ever was one that deserves to be so called, is for ever irrecoverable."

---

14) See *51 Reasons Why the King James* (Chick Publications 2018), page 154.

Kirsopp Lake trusted the "man-become-god" in Mark 1 of Codex Sinaiticus, instead of the true Son of God.

Three decades later, Sinaiticus photographer and scholar, Kirsopp Lake (1872-1946) echoed the same doubt: "In spite of the claims of Westcott and Hort and of Von Soden, we do not know the original form of the Gospels, and it is quite likely that we never shall."[15]

This confusion is all based on the doubting camp's refusal to accept the English Bible that was produced by the most eminent committee of scholars ever assembled, dedicated to an honest translation before God. The *un*faithful scholars have successfully twisted the conversation away from a solid trust in the one Bible that has historically produced strong faith in its readers, to many Bibles that leave Christians in a quagmire of doubt and confusion today, even in our "Bible-believing" churches.

Now when we hear the statement: "But I trust the scholars," we must ask the question: ***Which*** scholars are we talking about?

Why Another Bible?

English speaking people were presented in 1611 with a

---

15) See *Look What's Missing* (Chick Publications, 2009) pages 54-55.

preserved copy of God's words. Once we had that, we did not need another. Satan's subsequent con job, to "*fix* the King James" through the "science of textual criticism," has let him gleefully lead the masses into a mess of confusion and doubt.

Charles Spurgeon's prediction was indeed prophetic. He tried out the ERV for a time. But he soon saw the dangerous trap it led to. In the last sermon that he preached to pastors he said:

> "Believe in the inspiration of Scripture, and believe it in the most intense sense.... If this book be not infallible, where shall we find infallibility? ...Are these correctors of Scripture infallible? Is it certain that our Bibles are not right, but that the critics must be so? Now... when you have read your Bible, and have enjoyed its precious promises, you will have, to-morrow morning, to go down the street to ask the scholarly man at the parsonage whether this portion of the Scripture belongs to the inspired part of the Word, or whether it is of dubious authority.... All possibility of certainty is transferred from the spiritual man to a class of persons whose scholarship is pretentious... who do not even pretend to spirituality. We shall gradually be so bedoubted and becriticized, that only a few of the most profound will know what is the Bible, and what is not, and they will dictate to the rest of us. I have no more faith in their mercy than in their accuracy: they will rob us of all that we hold most dear...."

Spurgeon lived from 1834 to 1892. He saw firsthand how the Bible was being taken over in the scholars' scheme to "update" it. He clearly understood how the ungodly scholars had a corrupt agenda. To this day, doubting scholars known as Textual Critics have a field day arguing which parts of the text *might* be really what God said and what words, phrases and verses were added or taken away, whether intentionally or by accident. They can't answer anyone else's Bible questions, much less their own —simply because ***they have no standard.***

KJV Has A Solid History

It was an all-out assault on the King and the Bible he authorized. But the King James (the new name given to the English Bible) was not easily deposed. Beside Christ's assurance that He would preserve His words, over 5,700 manuscripts spread over 2 millennia have provided a solid foundation for its history. Because they were hand written, there were slight variations in the different copies. But aside from a very few verses, almost all the text has been remarkably resilient over the centuries.

Besides that, the believing scholars who translated and checked the King James were unassailable in both their faith and their scholarship. And the necessity for people of opposing theological backgrounds (Puritans vs. Church of England) to agree on a single reading for every verse took all personal bias out of the translation. And they were careful to translate the exact meaning of every word, or phrase, or verse in clear English words. This method is known as "formal equivalence." We can pretty much look at the English words and "see" the Hebrew and Greek right through it. They took seriously God's words:

> Deuteronomy 4:2 "Ye shall not add unto the word which I command you, neither shall ye diminish ought from it, that ye may keep the commandments of the LORD your God which I command you."

THE COUNTER-REFORMATION: A NEW KIND OF ATTACK

In modern times, translators changed the focus to cultural equivalents for Bible words, instead of communicating the meaning of the Bible words themselves. It is a looser approach, known as "dynamic equivalence." It's like a paraphrase, but it leaves much room for the guesses, personal biases and cultural adaptations of the translator. In *Why They Changed the Bible* I told about how in Latin America, sometimes their art substituted a guinea pig for a lamb! Jesus as the "guinea pig of God"? Obviously, there are inherent pitfalls with this approach. The formal equivalent translation of the King James translators assures us that we have what God said, without men changing its meaning to suit their opinions.

Proverbs 30:6 "Add thou not unto his words, lest he reprove thee, and thou be found a liar."

Day-to-day details of the creation of the King James Version are not widely known or available today. One of the best sources is an older book by Alexander McClure, entitled *Translators Revived: Biographical Notes of the KJV Bible Translators*. (Several versions are available on the internet.) McClure spent 20 years collecting biographical data on many of the scholars tasked by King James for this momentous effort. He also included a short history of the period prior to the King James.

God decided to produce an enduring Bible crafted in a classic English so solid that it would become the standard against the mutations of the language over time. Until 1500, most of the natives to England spoke French! In fact, English, up until the popularity of the KJV, was still a loose mixture of Old English, Gaelic, Germanic, Anglo-Saxon, and generous helpings of Latin. There was not a lot of English literature produced until the 1500s.

The King James changed all that. Even today, over 200 modern figures of speech can be traced through the language of the KJV. For example: a little bird told me, from Ecclesiastes 10:20, and "skin of my teeth" from Job 19:20.

Upon completion of the King James in 1611, several printing corrections followed, adjusting spellings and typefaces for better readability by the common man. Tyndale's goal of making the Bible available to every "boy that driveth the plough" was largely achieved.

For over 400 years now the KJV has been truly the standard English Bible. Those who believe that Jesus kept His promise by bringing us this Bible see no reason to update it. God saw that the work only needed to be done correctly once, in the classic, enduring English. All we need to do is become familiar with that classic English, so that none of the meaning is lost as English continues to morph.

Common folk today with a little instruction are able to understand the KJV Bible. (See *The King James Bible Companion* for definitions of the less familiar words in the KJV.)[16]

Modern tools of research have exposed a previously unknown history of the more recently discovered "older and better manuscripts." That's the term given mainly to the Sinaiticus and the Vaticanus codices (big books). I give more details in the books, ***Did the Catholic Church Give Us the Bible, Look What's Missing, Why They Changed the Bible*** and ***Is the World's Oldest Bible a Fake?***[17]

Bait and Switch

The doubting scholars and Bible Societies gave the

---

16) *The King James Bible Companion* (Chick Publications, 2000)
17) *Is the World's Oldest Bible a Fake?* (Chick Publications, 2009)

THE COUNTER-REFORMATION: A NEW KIND OF ATTACK

impression they wanted to "fix" the King James. But it turns out that what they really wanted was to replace the KJV with a text of their liking. The replacement text, of course, had nothing in common with the thousands of manuscripts that we know support the KJV. Instead, they wanted a "doubting text," one that reflected their own doubts about what God said, if He said anything at all. The result is a Bible that leaves the reader so confused that he is not sure *what* God meant to say.

About the time of the first Bible Societies, the Western World was enamored with the new teachings of the Enlightenment. They taught that man, through science and reason, could figure out truth without God's involvement. This led to what was called "the science of textual criticism." This was quickly adopted by those who were intent on taking down the King James. Here's the result: when we say we trust the scholars who gave us the modern versions, we are really turning from faith in God's words and placing it in the popular representatives of the godless school of the Enlightenment.

If you were the Devil, how would you get people to disregard over 99.5% of the evidence (right now about 5,700 Greek Bible manuscripts) and fall for a made-up text, based mainly on just two big books? Add to that the fact that one of them, Vaticanus, only showed up in the Vatican's library about 1475, and nobody got to see it much until 1867. And the other one, Sinaiticus, was the project of a revolutionary monk, with the help of his great-nephew in 1839-40? Easy. Just make the doubting scholars think they were the greatest thing since sliced bread.

But how would you do that? First, you'd have to convince them of the lie that "older = better." Then, you'd have to get them to believe these manuscripts were "older and better" than anything they've ever seen. Maybe even say that they were as old as Constantine, in the early to mid-300s AD. Then you'd talk up the type of Greek text, as if it were better than anyone else's, especially since it was made by *scholars* like themselves! That would butter them up! Nothing appeals to pride more than feeling you know better than those around you.

So all those *other* manuscripts were made by commoners, not "brilliant intellectuals" like them.

At this point, the modern scholars were as intimidated as church mice. They wouldn't *dare* doubt the age or the quality of those manuscripts. They'd defend them like they'd defend their own careers!

And that, Brothers and Sisters, is exactly what happened.

The Bizarre "Byzantine" Plan

Even against common sense, all manuscripts that are like the King James, regardless of their actual age, are labeled "Byzantine," as if they were a compromised text. And what if the Bible text was older than the Byzantine period? Easy. They'd just say their "spurious reading" was ahead of its time!

This is no joke. That's how we got to where we are. By the 1960s, many Bible societies, who had compromised with Rome all the way back to the early 1800s, insisted that the Sinaiticus/Vaticanus Westcott and Hort-type text would be the only one allowed for translating the Bible worldwide.

I've shown in other books evidence of the thousands of discrepancies between the different versions now on the market. That happened because these doubting scholars could never agree on which words, phrases and verses belonged in the Bible, in crucial, even doctrinal passages. And though they disagreed, we were encouraged to trust our favorite, all-knowing scholarly text critic, who would sort it all out for us.

Chapter 11

Motives Of The Scholars Behind The Modern Bible Versions

I once visited Claremont Theological Seminary's library for a Bible college project, looking up old articles in journals on the Greek word "eis." While there, I accidentally walked to the wrong rack. I picked up the huge journal binder for a year in the 1960s. And I found a familiar scholar's name and article! I was so intrigued to see what he wrote, apart from all the stuff our teachers were telling us about him. He introduced the article by telling that back when he was 10 years old, he used to pray to God. But now he doesn't pray any longer.

I was crestfallen. I was dumbfounded. But he's a New Testament Bible scholar! Yes, he was. But he had zero faith. He said so in the introduction to this article, which no doubt was the transcript of a speech to the theological society. Then he proceeded to reinterpret Pauls' Epistle to the Romans as if it were written by Plato!

I never looked at theologians the same again. And that was 1982.

From that day forward, only one year into Bible college, I viewed all scholarly writings as being written by adversaries, not people on my side. And I kept my faith, because I determined back then I would trust what God said, above any theologian, scholar, friend or enemy.

I was living out the scripture God gave me that first night of my repentance, August 24, 1980: Psalm 118:8-9 *It is better to trust in the LORD than to put confidence in man. It is better to trust in the LORD than to put confidence in princes.*

And that scripture would bail me out of serious situations more times after that, as well.

Since this is a book to help us understand what we mean when we say: "But I trust the scholars," let's recap from that perspective.

So far, we have established that many of the leaders in the Bible were scholars, people whose deep learning was used by the Holy Ghost to produce enduring works of scripture, Bible literature and translations.

We also noted that, in spite of much learning, scholars' agendas often include a wide variety of motives. In other words, learning does not guarantee righteousness. And from the beginning, we could identify two basic agendas, one to promote faith in God's words, and the other effectively designed to inspire doubt.

So, let's take a look at the men behind the new Bible text and examine their agendas.

Revision Committees

Since the beginning of the effort to "fix" the King James, the Revision Committees have placed themselves in charge of the details. It is important to look at the people who make up these societies and examine their agendas.

The best way to do that is to look at the people who produced the first "revision" of the King James —really a non-King

James Bible. The New Testament was published in 1881 and the whole Bible minus Apocrypha in 1885. [Footnote: Most don't know it, but they actually published the Apocrypha for the Revised Version in 1895.] It was simply called the Revised Version or English Revised Version and was published by Oxford University Press and Thomas Nelson Publishers.

Its Old Testament portion was based on the Masoretic Text, though it was re-translated. However, its New Testament was based on a brand-new Greek text *with* its roots in the Alexandrian stream of manuscripts.[18]

Here the plot thickens considerably.

The new Greek text was put together by scholars Westcott and Hort. Their product was the result of a complex and very successful maneuver to sideline and discredit the King James Bible.

With considerable tacit approval from the Vatican, who already had had the Vaticanus on file since 1475, [Footnote: There are many codices called "Vaticanus." This one is called "Vaticanus 1209.] scholar Constantin Tischendorf was credited with finding another "ancient" manuscript, the Sinaiticus, in the St. Catherine's Monastery in Egypt.

The "Science" of Paleography

These two incomplete copies of the Bible in Greek were paraded as better examples of what God said than the hugely supported manuscript history of the King James translation. The two codices were identified as "very ancient" by the so-called science of Paleography, a highly subjective method of dating manuscripts invented by a couple of French monks.

---

18) The new Greek text was released it just one week before the New Testament in English.

Tischendorf's training in Paleography was how he was able to make the claim that the Sinaiticus originated in the 300s AD, even when it had zero verifiable history.[19]

The Vaticanus magically appeared in the Vatican library in 1475, yet it was also declared ancient by the "Paleographers," and became, along with its pseudo-sister Sinaiticus, the foundation manuscripts for Westcott and Hort's new and improved Greek text. This text was then adopted by the revision committee to replace the King James.

This, then, is how the first "Revision," the English Revised Version of 1881-1885, came into being, followed by its sibling, the American Standard Version of 1901. These two versions, masquerading as revisions, marked the beginning of the flood of Bibles now available on the market, all of which are based on the questionable Westcott and Hort text and the later Nestle texts adapted from it.

An "Interconfessional" World Text

In 1966, with the help of scholar Eugene Nida, all Protestant and Roman Catholic Bible Societies came to agreement on a single "interconfessional" Greek text to be used by all future missionary translators, as well as all new modern English Bible translations. They also agreed that anytime a Bible was produced for a people who had a Roman Catholic culture, the Apocrypha would be included.

This universal Greek text ignored what is now a 5,700+ manuscript history supporting the King James. This history had been swept under the rug and re-labeled "Byzantine." This effectively nullified the whole history of the preserved Bibles, including the King James. The omissions described in *Look*

---

19) For more details, see *Is the World's Oldest Bible a Fake?*

What's Missing are included in the interconfessional master text.

All modern translations are either derived from this "critical" Greek text, or they have footnotes that list their changed words and meanings as an option for Bible readers to "make up their own mind" (meaning, doubt God's words). My book, ***Why They Changed the Bible,*** describes a key maneuver during the so-called "updating" of the KJV.[20]

Just one man, Eugene Nida, was responsible for a major shift in the method used in Bible translation work. As referred to above, *dynamic equivalence* theory came to replace *formal equivalence* as used by the KJV translators. Formal equivalence is, basically, an attempt to find an exact word or phrase in the new language to match the meaning of the word in its context, from the original language. Exact word-for-word is not always possible. That's why the goal is to exactly convey the original meaning.

Dynamic equivalence seeks to adapt the original meaning to the thinking and culture of the prospective reader. There are examples of the results from the benign to the absurd. One missionary, using dynamic equivalence decided to translate the Bible word, "temple" as "longhouse," since that was the central place of worship for his particular tribe. That sounds fair, until you realize that a longhouse was used for ancestral spirit worship! In this day of computers and internet, there is no excuse for not showing them the actual, Biblical objects.

In *Why They Changed the Bible,* I cite another example where the "Lamb" of God was replaced with the "Guinea Pig" of God because sheep were not known to that tribe and the

---

20) Today, some of these "doubting footnotes" are even included in new editions of the KJV.

Guinea pig was central to their pagan sacrificial system. The book contains pictures of a painting of the last supper with the Guinea pig dead on a plate where the lamb is supposed to be. Modern English versions use this method to some degree. More extreme examples are *The Message* and *The Cotton Patch Gospels*.

Nida was not only key in swinging both English and foreign translation procedures over to the dynamic equivalence method. He also spent his life promoting the "interconfessional" text that would be acceptable to both Roman Catholics and pushed on all varieties of Protestants.

Chapter 12

Real World Seminary Scholars

The sad truth about modern scholarship hit me personally when I went to Fuller Seminary. I had seen unbelieving teachings in books. But nothing prepared me for having Bible-doubters as my own professors.

It was so different from the way I view --pretty much everything.

God's words are *alive*. When I approach the Bible, I approach *HIS* Book. They're not my words. They're His. That is what makes this holy book so wonderful. I can always go to God, in His word, and I can find out what my heavenly Father *thinks*, what He *wants*, and *what will make Him happy*.

But here is what my professors at Fuller Seminary said. And remember, this was considered one of the most conservative seminaries, and second biggest in the country when I studied there from 1984-87.

Let me introduce you to some of the scholars in residence, my Fuller professors.

This is Dan Fuller, son of the founder, Charles Fuller. (It was a sermon by Charles Fuller that Jack Chick heard and was so convicted he got saved right there and then, on his honeymoon!)

How far the apple fell from the tree! Dan taught Unity of the Bible with huge syllabi we had to buy. His system of Bible arcs said that after the Fall of man in Genesis 3, God didn't talk in person to His creation anymore. But as I said then, God's right there talking with Cain in the very next chapter, Genesis 4! Dr. Fuller never changed his notes to match the Bible. His mind was made up.

This is Paul Jewett. He taught us that Adam didn't find a companion until he looked and saw one of the apes. He said, and I quote, "That one over there. I think it's something in the eyes." So, Dr. Jewett, this champion of women as pastors, taught that the first woman was literally an ape!

This is Dr. Ralph P. Martin. He changed the meaning of a couple of Greek words in Acts 1, as I said in *Why They Changed the Bible*. I pointed out in front of the class that his changed meaning would make it like Luke and Acts were written in the 2nd century, contradicting the Bible, which says Luke was an eyewitness. He leaned over on his microphone, and responded to me before a couple hundred students: "Well, THAT wouldn't hurt your faith, would it?"

This is Dr. Lewis B. Smedes. He liked to tear down the faith of each individual class member in the 10 Commandments like a confrontational talk-show host. He'd make up tear-jerking scenarios, where breaking a commandment seemed like the only thing you could do, to solve the problem he made up. And when someone finally broke down, emotionally, he would say, "So you don't *really* believe in that commandment, do you?" He took pleasure in tearing people's faith into shreds.

These are Drs. Hubbard, LaSor and Bush. They wrote an Old Testament Introduction text that said Ezekiel wanted to make a bigger temple. But alas, his plans didn't work out. (That's Ezekiel 40-48). They said that those chapters were simply Ezekiel's wish-fulfillment dream, not from God. They believed the Bible was written by man, not inspired by God.

David Allan Hubbard was president of Fuller, and my Hebrew Literature professor. William Sanford LaSor was also my Hebrew readings professor. Frederick Bush was another Old Testament professor.

Dr. Bob Schaper, who was also my homiletics (not preaching) professor, came into Bush's class and said two things:

1. If we had a Polaroid camera, we would not have seen God forming man of the dust of the ground and breathing into his nostrils the breath of life.

2. If we had a Polaroid camera, we would not have seen Jesus ascend to heaven. "Heaven isn't up," he said.

But Acts 1 says Jesus went up *before their eyes*, while they watched. But Dr. Schaper never let the facts get in the way of his beliefs.

 Dr. Donald Hagner, one of my New Testament professors, who always read straight from the United Bible Society's Greek text to us, believed that many of Paul's letters were written after Paul died by somebody else who faked his name. That means he believed these New Testament books would be Pseudepigrapha, "false writings."

Oh, and one more thing. All the professors here, as far as they have said and I was told, were evolutionists. They thought the story of Creation was a fairy tale, and Genesis chapters 1-11 was just poetry.

These guys trained thousands of present pastors and professors when they went to seminary, as I did. And they are only the *conservative* tip of the iceberg.

Should I trust these scholars, simply because they are scholars? Does what they believe matter? You bet! Despite the fact that they lifted up Sinaiticus and Vaticanus before us in the classroom, not one single professor came to class and cradled the text of **Codex Sinaiticus** in his arms and said, "At last! THESE are the words of God!"

Not even Dr. Paul Jewett, who went to Vatican II, (and made sure we knew about it), not even he held his copy of **Codex Vaticanus** in his arms and said, "*Now* we have God's holy words!"

Not one of them showed **any** evidence of a passionate belief in the *living* words of God.

A lot of Fuller graduates teach in conservative Bible colleges. Did they teach *your* pastor?

Chapter 13

Summary

Today, we have one English Bible, supported by over 5,700 manuscripts with a unique unity of text and message. It was translated by faithful and competent men, dedicated to communicating the very words that Jesus had promised to preserve.

On the other hand, we have dozens of modern bibles loosely translated by doubting scholars using dynamic equivalence from a single, modern critical text based primarily on two manuscripts of questionable origin. And when we examine the credentials and reputations of the modern Bible scholars, there is much concern about their agenda.

Most of the scholars of this variety testify to their doubt of Christ's promise to preserve His words by claiming that we no longer have trustworthy records of His words. They have built their careers as *textual critics,* debating endlessly which words we should believe as God's ultimate truth.

To us, it is unthinkable that anyone would mess with THE BIBLE! Yet, Satan has made it a central focus of his rebellion against his Creator, to try to raise doubt about what God said. His first question to Eve was: "Yea, hath God said?" And it paid off, big time! Why should we think that he has given up? We know that he wins some and loses some. But should we not be keenly watching for where he might be winning?

When I researched and wrote the books mentioned above,

it exposed a monstrous plot right under our noses. His string of lies are as long as your arm. But the central lie for us today is that the King James Version needs "fixing."

The second lie was that its text and its language were outdated. The third lie was that their fake "ancient" manuscripts were "better." Fourth was the lie that the King James Bible is worthless: "Who wants to read those old "thees" and "thous?"

Then there was the lie that because there is so much confusion in the new versions, only a scholar or pastor-scholar can figure out what God said. Except he can't *really* do it, because we don't know what the original autographs said. That would put us in quite a mess, wouldn't it?

So an unbelieving set of scholars bought this string of lies, creating the huge, lucrative Bible market.

But the other, believing variety of scholars had already given us a solid Bible in classic English, currently supported by over 5,700 coherent manuscripts. They believed that they were working with the preserved words of God and handing them on in plowboy English. God blessed this Bible with 400 years of good fruit. There is no actual evidence that God has blessed **any** subsequent effort in English.

What we have today are dozens of widely differing Bibles built on the opinions of men, who disregarded the very documents God spent all that time preserving for us. I pity the man who trusts in men. Look at what God said:

Jeremiah 17:5 "Thus saith the LORD; Cursed be the man that trusteth in man, and maketh flesh his arm, and whose heart departeth from the LORD."

Psalms 118:8-9 "It is better to trust in the LORD than to

put confidence in man. It is better to trust in the LORD than to put confidence in princes."

Our trust must rest in God Himself. Then we must trust what He has revealed. That is why He gave us the scriptures in the first place.

I pity the man who is taught to believe that **he** replaces the scriptures as the authority.

Once you let go of the scriptures as your anchor, you are subject to every wind of doctrine. It almost sounds like a Bible verse.

Ephesians 4:14 "That we henceforth be no more children, tossed to and fro, and carried about with every *wind of doctrine*, by the sleight of men, and cunning craftiness, whereby they lie in wait to deceive;"

And how do we get correct doctrine?

> 2 Timothy 3:16-17 "All scripture is given by inspiration of God, and is profitable for doctrine, for reproof, for correction, for instruction in righteousness: That the man of God may be perfect, throughly furnished unto all good works."

The word makes the scholar perfect. The scholar doesn't make the word perfect.

It was many years ago at Chick Publications when I first saw the books that said the new versions were bad. As I read the books, I thought they were absurd. I thought they were ignorant. And I soon trashed them all and turned back to my NIV, NRSV, NAS, and New King James. They were all considered more "scholarly," by my professors in Bible college and Fuller Seminary.

Now, when someone defends his use of the modern Bibles by expressing his trust in the scholars, you can decide whether

SUMMARY

to challenge his misplaced faith. You will have to calculate whither you might be subjected to the same ridicule as the many saintly scholars who have defended the preservation of God's words in history.

Two types of scholars, two agendas. Bible-believing scholars believe the Bible over their own opinions.

The other kind of scholars believe their own opinions over the Bible.

There is no middle ground.

There are two types of scholars in the world: ***which are YOU going to trust?***

ALSO BY **DAVID W. DANIELS**

112 pages, paperback

Before you buy another Bible, look at what's being left out!

- See how one left-out word makes Jesus a liar in 19 modern Bibles!
- See which entire verse was removed to leave room for infant baptism.
- See the verses where adultery is removed from God's sin list.
- Does your Bible warn of hell? Many don't!

ALSO BY **DAVID W. DANIELS**

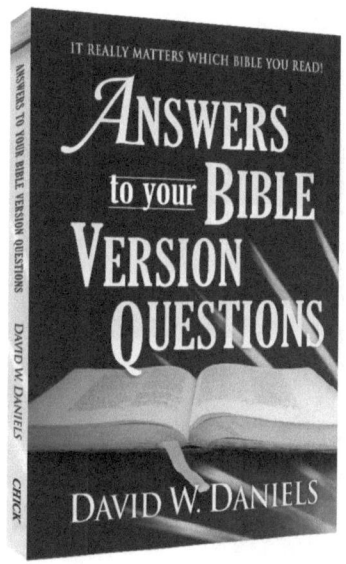

224 pages, paperback

If you believe God preserved His words, where can you find them?

History shows that there are two streams of Bible texts, and they are not the same. Obviously, both of them cannot be correct.

Respected linguist David W. Daniels proves beyond a doubt how we can know the King James Bible is God's preserved words in English. He answers many of the difficult questions the so-called "experts" throw against the King James.

Whether you want to defend the King James Bible or learn which Bible you can trust, you will find the answers here.

ALSO BY **DAVID W. DANIELS**

224 pages, paperback

Are there reasons to trust that God kept His promise to preserve His own words? Yes! There are many. This book is a small collection of those.

People have been finding not only what faith looks like, but have actually made the move and left the doubting Bibles, with their contradictory doctrines, and come to the King James. There they found a consistent message, consistent doctrine, and a consistent faith.

So they can hold the Bible up in their hands and say, "Thus saith the Lord! This is the words of God."

ALSO BY **DAVID W. DANIELS**

352 pages, paperback

Publishers are making significant changes to match an "old" Bible called the "Sinaiticus." In this book, David W. Daniels proves the Sinaiticus is a 19th century hoax with easy-to-understand evidence.

Why are they doing it? To change the Bible text to one that can accept everyone's doctrine, to be One World Bible for One World Church.

ALSO BY **DAVID W. DANIELS**

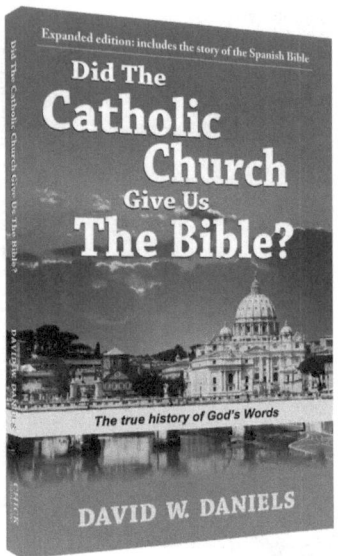

208 pages, paperback

Expanded edition includes history of Spanish Bible.

The Bible has two histories. One is of God preserving His words through His people. The other is of the devil using Roman Catholic "scholars" to pervert God's words and give us corrupt modern Bibles.

Read the history of not one, but two Bibles... One that matches centuries of evidence, and another that has been changed to justify Catholic doctrine.

Made in United States
Troutdale, OR
08/21/2024

22218675R00046